JAPANESE
COST MANAGEMENT

JAPANESE COST MANAGEMENT

MICHIHARU SAKURAI
D. PAUL SCARBROUGH

CRISP PUBLICATIONS

Editor-in-Chief: *William F. Christopher*

Managing Editor: *Kathleen Barcos*

Editor: *Follin Armfield*

Cover Design: *Kathleen Barcos*

Cover Production: *Russell Leong Design*

Book Design & Production: *London Road Design*

Printer: *Bawden Printing*

Library of Congress Card Catalog Number 97-65795

ISBN 1-56052-435-9

Contents

ABBREVIATIONS
USED IN THE BOOK

ABC	Activity-Based Costing
ABM	Activity-Based Management
AMT	Advanced Manufacturing Technology
CAD	Computer-Aided Design
CAE	Computer-Aided Engineering
CAM	Computer-Aided Manufacturing
CIM	Computer-Integrated Manufacturing
DCOPLS	Direct Charge of Overhead to Product Line System
FA	Factory Automation
FMS	Flexible Manufacturing System
IKM	Innovation–Kaizen–Maintenance
IRR	Internal Rate of Return
JIT	Just-In-Time
NC	Numerical Control (Machine)
NPV	Net Present Value
OA	Office Automation
POS	Point of Sale
R&D	Research and Development
ROI	Return on Investment
ROS	Return on Sales
TPM	Total Productivity Maintenance
TQC	Total Quality Control
VA	Value Analysis
VE	Value Engineering

I.

COST MANAGEMENT APPROACHES
OF THE JAPANESE

B Y ALTERNATELY LEARNING FROM and then chal-
lenging the West, Japan has provided many of the
world's business innovations since the 1970s. In
this book we describe four new accounting tools from
Japan for cost management and, equally important, we
describe the five business practice innovations and four
cost engineering tools that make the accounting tools
work. Since the cost management practices we describe
have their roots in the business culture, this first chapter
illustrates some of the important changes in Japanese business since the 1960s. Failure to understand the roots of the
new Japanese tools is one of the main reasons these tools
often fail in the West.

One of the main problems Westerners have when
studying the Japanese is that they study the business techniques without realizing how inextricably tied they are to
the culture. In this book we bridge the gap by presenting
context as an integral part of the tool. We start by focusing
on the changes in Japan's business environment.

A Framework for Current Management Accounting in Japan

After having experienced process automation in the 1960s, the Japanese began to move aggressively into factory automation. The impetus came from the declining birth rate and resulting shrinkage in number of available employees. Pushed by the change in demographics, Japanese companies made their major investments in automation based not on financial considerations—but on survival needs. Without automation they could not continue to make products in Japan! As a result, they encountered and broke through the limits of conventional cost management earlier and more forcefully than most Western firms. The changes from traditional to flexible manufacturing systems (FMS) to factory automation (FA) and later to computer-integrated manufacturing (CIM) demanded dramatic improvements to management accounting. The Japanese responded to this challenge by developing unique management accounting tools such as target costing and cost engineering tools such as just-in-time (JIT).

The Japan Accounting Association revealed many of the newest developments in its influential book, *Integrated Cost Management* (Sakurai et al., 1993). The key concept is that of integrated cost management (ICM), defined as a comprehensive *value chain* approach to strategic cost management for products, software and services. This includes the entire *product life cycle* from research and development (R&D) to product planning, design, manufacturing, sales promotion, physical distribution, operation, maintenance

Description	1960s	1990s
Business Environment	Exports Mass production [low-variety, high-volume] Industrialization	Globalization Flexible production [high-variety, low-volume] Computerization
Corporate Mission	Profit	Survival, Growth, and Development
Corporate Goals	Profitability	Effectiveness
Operating Doctrine	Planning and Control	IKM + Planning and Control
Organizational Structure	Functional	Cross-functional + Functional
Functional Areas using Management Accounting	Production and Marketing	R&D, Planning and Design, Marketing, Operations, Maintenance, and Disposal
Industries using Management Accounting Tools	Manufacturing	Manufacturing, Service, and Software
Main Tools Used	Standard Costing Budgeting Variable Costing Operations Research [OR] Industrial Engineering [IE] Others	All the tools of the 1960s + Target Costing ABC and ABM Quality Costing Life-cycle Management TQC, TPM, JIT, VE Others

Figure 1. **Management accounting in the 1960s and 1990s**
Adapted from: Sakurai, Michiharu, and Paul Scarbrough, Integrated
Cost Management, *Productivity Press 1995. Used with permission.*

and disposal. It is expected that cost reductions and quality improvements, across the life cycle and value chain, will provide the highest overall benefit. That is, the most effective cost management operates at the strategic level. Figure 1 shows the typical philosophy and techniques in the 1960s and 1990s.

In addition to the demographic shift, Japan has few resources and has suffered a series of jarring economic shocks starting with the oil crisis in the early 1970s. Since

Japan must import all factors of production except labor, a company's cost structure depends on the international market prices for commodities—a highly volatile system. As a result, the Japanese are much more aware of the strategic implications of cost management than most Western firms.

Responding to the above factors, Japanese management has gradually divorced itself from predominantly U.S.-derived methods to create a distinctively Japanese approach. This change has penetrated so deep as to include the general business approach, organizational structure, major areas of accounting activity and accounting techniques. Although the Japanese approach is unique and part of its own cultural matrix, we can learn many lessons. In the following sections we identify five major innovations in business practice, four new accounting tools, and four cost engineering tools.

General Business Approach
or Operating Doctrine

IKM Operating Doctrine

INNOVATION 1. The implicit contract between employee and employer has been changed.

Planning and control systems are indispensable in societies where a command-and-control orientation prevails, such as the United States. However, Japanese firms have redefined the employee obligation to consist of what

4

Sakurai and Scarbrough (1995) call innovation, kaizen, and maintenance (IKM). This framework alters the structure of the job and organization of the company as well as profoundly transforming the implicit labor contract between the organization and the employee. IKM is not a change in technique, but a change in culture.

In this context, innovation means that a basic responsibility of an employee is to develop innovative changes to products or production processes as a result of introducing new technology and/or investing in plant and equipment. It is the result of discontinuous discovery activities and is radical in its effect. Kaizen is the employee's responsibility for continuously improving current activities. It includes not only daily, small continuous improvement, but also changes in management structure. Maintenance means the employee has responsibility for maintaining current standards in technology, business and operations. The traditional view of employee responsibility would be only "maintenance."

This change from the traditional "planning and control" perspective to IKM may be the most significant piece of the puzzle for U.S. businesses attempting to use Japanese methods. It is not widely known that IKM attitudes are the necessary driving force behind the Japanese cost engineering tools such as JIT, total productivity maintenance (TPM), total quality control (TQC), and value engineering (VE).

Uniquely, the IKM approach is explicitly purposive, from the three names (IKM) to the language it uses, while the planning and control approach is not. Our traditional planning and control approach implicitly assumes that

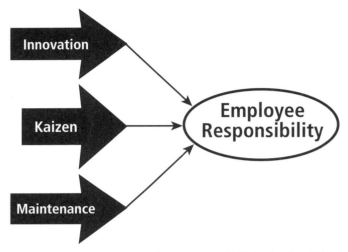

Figure 2. Japanese employee responsibilities in the 1990s

the purpose of the organization flows from upper-level managers, and that the tools and their users are somewhat detached professional service providers. None of the many U.S. tools such as standard costing, operating budgets, variable costing, or capital expenditure budgets implies *improvement* in any business function—only planning and control. In fact, it would be possible to have a perfectly functioning system using those techniques and still have no effective improvements or even *attempts* at improvements.

The framework of IKM fits Japanese companies in using TQC, JIT, TPM and target costing better than the traditional framework of planning and control because IKM tools are also purposive—each seeks not to discipline its subject, but to change its nature. The purpose of TQC is to improve quality. The purpose of JIT is to reduce inventory. The purpose of TPM is to improve machine availability. The purpose of target costing is to reduce product cost. The IKM operating doctrine and the Japanese tools probably developed together, but even if they did not, they are mutually supportive. In fact, many failures of North American companies to succeed with the Japanese cost engineering tools may come from the lack of reinforcement and direction provided by the IKM operating doctrine.

Organizational Structure

INNOVATION 2. Pervasive use of cross-functional work groups.

Cross-functional work groups change the way the Japanese operate. In the past, the structure of the business organization was based on functions such as production, marketing, purchasing, R&D, engineering, personnel and accounting. Even today this functional organization is essential because of the specialized knowledge base each area develops. The functional areas provide the reservoir of expertise needed for success. In addition, however, cross-functional structures have become indispensable for developing new products or conducting R&D because *they express strategic imperatives at the operating level.* These cross-functional structures are important because they allow the cooperative work of each area to influence other areas, as well as allowing tradeoffs in cost between areas.

In many instances this influence occurs informally. The information density in each functional area, however, has increased dramatically and, at the same time, increased physical and organizational distances make communication more difficult. To ensure that the cross-functional activity takes place, even in the face of obstacles, most Japanese companies create formal work groups with a cross-functional structure that co-exist with the traditional functional structures.

INNOVATION 3. Japanese firms practice job rotation across functional boundaries.

High-profile Japanese firms rotate management employees across functional areas throughout their careers. By the time they are in mid-career, most have had extensive experience in accounting, finance, marketing and production. This experience helps them function very effectively in cross-functional teams. The broader experience that they have gives them an ability to envision the value chain and make tradeoffs that are strategically consistent with the company's mission. Taken together, the cross-functional work groups and forced job rotation reinforce, and may even have caused, the development of Japanese CIM and the value chain approach.

Major Arenas for Management Accounting

INNOVATION 4. Use of managerial accounting in new functional areas and in different industries.

In the past, management accounting was used mainly in production, marketing and, in some cases, finance functions. It is used in many other areas now. Currently, management accounting is used in R&D; product planning and design; and such life-cycle planning areas as operations, maintenance and disposal. Due to many features of Japanese business this has not increased the numbers of accountants, as might be expected in the United States. Instead, managerial accounting has become a responsibility of all managers. In the past, management accounting was used mainly in the manufacturing industries. Currently, it is also used extensively in the computer software, telecommunications, merchandising and other service industries.

INNOVATION 5. Use of ROS as a strategic goal.

In high-technology companies, return on sales (ROS) rather than return on investment (ROI) has been used increasingly for the corporate profit goal. ROS can be used strategically when it is used along with efficient tools for reducing inventory such as JIT or target costing. Increasingly, leading Japanese companies do not typically use ROI.

Individually, any one of these five innovations would be important. Taken together, they have an incalculable effect on Japanese business and strategic effectiveness. As we will see later on, attempting to use specific Japanese techniques without the underlying support offered by these five innovations dramatically reduces the chances of success. In the next section you will see some of the accounting and cost engineering methods that arose from this Japanese business environment.

Major Management Accounting Techniques

In the 1960s and 1970s, Japanese companies used traditional management accounting techniques such as standard costing, operating budgets, variable costing and capital expenditure budgeting in almost the same way as did U.S. companies. This use was the result of an active introduction of U.S. management accounting systems after World War II.

Today, the Japanese have added a set of new tools to the managerial accounting palette. These include:

1. Target costing

2. Kaizen costing

3. Cost tables

4. Middle-range planning

So far, these new tools have been used most intensively in assembly-oriented industries although they are spreading fast. The following familiar cost engineering tools are usually used at the same time.

1. Total Quality Control (TQC)

2. Just-In-Time (JIT)

3. Total Productivity Maintenance (TPM)

4. Value Engineering (VE)

The cost engineering tools are regarded as distinct from, but coherent with, managerial accounting. These last four cost engineering tools are not discussed much in this book, since many business people are familiar with them and the business press carries good descriptions of them.

The cauldron of disruptive changes we call the move to factory automation is where the five business practice innovations, accounting tools and cost engineering tools became a coherent doctrine. We need to know more about the move to FA and CIM before looking in detail at the accounting tools. So in the next chapter we will discuss the impact of FA and CIM on Japanese business management and accounting methods.

II.

FA, CIM and Their Impact on Business Management

F OR MANAGEMENT ACCOUNTANTS the most important changes in the last few decades have resulted
from the rapid movement to more automated and
integrated business methods. These new methods wreak
havoc on managerial accounting forms of analysis because
they violate the unspoken assumptions in the traditional
techniques. For example, traditional production accounting
methods assume that direct labor drives most costs, yet we
know this does not happen in factory automation (FA).
The new environment also violates other assumptions,
such as the little recognized fact that standard costing
is useful for control purposes in situations with low to
medium amounts of variability, but not in situations
with high variability or the extremely low variability
we see in advanced manufacturing technology (AMT).

As a result of such changes, some methods lose their
main purpose entirely. One example of this is standard
costing, which exists mainly to control direct labor in mass
production or medium-variability environments. As we

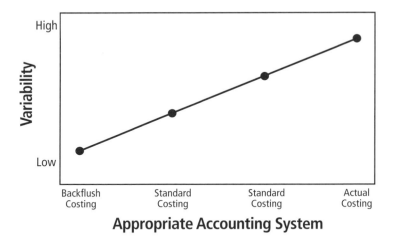

Figure 3. **Standard costing and variability**

will see later, however, losing the main purpose does not mean that the technique disappears; in AMT even more companies use standard costing than ever—to make it easier to prepare financial statements.

Japanese managers who face advanced manufacturing technology now find themselves searching for new methods of business management more suitable for FA and CIM. They do so from within their experience in the Japanese business culture, which we look at below.

Background Information on FA

Why did Japan create the massive innovation in FA in the 1980s? No one knows exactly, of course, but here are a few of the factors commonly thought to have been involved:

1. Most of the blame should probably go to the labor shortage. Japan reached zero population growth (i.e., total fertility rate was 2.0) in 1975, and shows signs of a devastating decline (i.e., total fertility rate in 1994 was 1.50). Japanese business strategists have been planning for severe and permanent labor shortages since the middle 1970s. In this scenario FA is *not* a business opportunity, but a much lower-level survival priority. The need to reduce labor use becomes more focused as the shortage expands up the skill ladder to include a scarcity of engineers and skilled workers.

2. Increased resistance to hard, dirty and dangerous jobs among young workers. The younger generation wants to work in banks, insurance companies, consulting firms and other similar organizations.

3. The rapid fluctuations in the exchange rage (for example, one U.S. dollar brought 360 yen before the 1960s, 260 yen in 1975, 127 yen in 1988, and 80 yen in mid-1995).

4. Pressure placed on Japan by the newly industrialized countries in Asia.

Taking these factors together, we can see that they created the conditions of possibility which enabled Japanese managers to justify the investment in what was then such a *financially* risky strategy. In a situation with some similarities, U.S. managers seem to lean more heavily toward off-shore production. We have no hypotheses as to why, although it is obvious that the overall business environment is very different in the two countries.

Then Again, What Is FA, Really?

Although we use terms for automation such as FA and CIM as if they were well understood, they are not. So in this section we will define what we mean by these words.

In the United States, the term FMS (flexible manufacturing systems) describes the automation of factories, and more recently we see the term CIM (computer-integrated manufacturing) used. In Japan, however, the term FA has been widely adopted as the all-inclusive term describing the automation of factories. It refers to a coherent automation of a factory that extends to the entire factory and includes such things as technology, design, the flow of materials, and the central computer systems, as well as the flexibility to cope with the production of a variety of products in medium and small volume, as distinguished from process automation.

Although FA can have many variations, in this book it means the integration of flexible manufacturing systems (FMS), which integrates industrial robots, numerical control (NC) machines, and unmanned vehicles (using the concepts of cellular manufacturing), with computer-aided design (CAD), computer-aided manufacturing (CAM), computer-aided engineering (CAE), and office automation (OA) of the factory. Building on top of this, CIM expands FA to integrate manufacturing, engineering and marketing

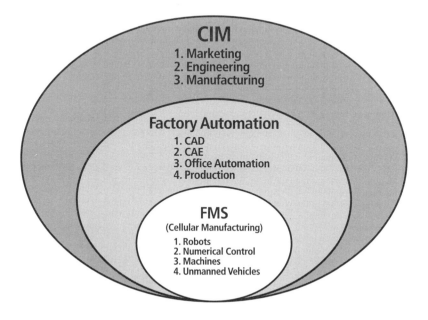

Figure 4. How CIM relates business areas

through computer networks. Figure 4 shows a diagram of FA relationship.

Flexible Manufacturing Systems

FMS provides the heart of FA. It combines two components: automation of movement (traditional automation) and automation of setups (Numerically Controlled [NC] machines).

Transfer machines and specialized machinery systems increase productivity of mass-produced products, but they lack flexibility.

Numerically Controlled machines can change over quite rapidly to a different item (rapid setups) in high-variety/low-volume production. But they have difficulty achieving high volumes.

The combination of the two results in FMS. Since flexibility has become more necessary, various peripheral devices such as automatic conveyors and automatic warehouses are arranged around NC machine tools and industrial robots—all managed by a computer-controlled central system. This arrangement tends to give greater overall productivity and flexibility in the production process.

Computer-Aided Design, Manufacturing and Engineering

Automation of a factory does not stop at automation of the production system. The complexity of many high-technology products has made the engineering drawings much more complex, as well as increasing the number of drawings needed. Hence, CAD has become necessary to increase precision, quality and speed of design.

Office Automation

OA is a system designed to increase efficiency of office work in two respects: (1) reducing the labor devoted to clerical tasks, and (2) supporting creative operations. Productivity in office work had hitherto been backward in comparison with manufacturing productivity in major Japanese companies. Through automation of office work, the paperless factory has become a realistic goal. As a result of standardization efforts, the preparation of documents related to production, management accounting operations, communications and storage operations has become more efficient. At the same time, in order to provide support for creative tasks, computer and communications systems provide communication methods such as teleconferencing, electronic mail, electronic commerce, electronic data interchange, and means for accessing the most pertinent information, as well as modes for analysis and processing.

Here we do not mean OA in the narrow sense of introducing personal computers or word processors. Rather it means the broader chain of activities that increase the productivity of white-collar tasks and increase the productivity of such overall operations in the factory as managing delivery times, quality control and control of costs. It contains some of the concepts and activities now popularized under the banner of business process reengineering.

The Emergence of CIM

In the 1990s, the diversification of the market and the need for individualized products has become more intense. To compete, the business strategy dictated both greater variety and more new products. This is only possible with very tight linkages between marketing, design, production, and the customer. For example, point of sale (POS) technology expands the marketing link to include the customer. Conceptually, this links market information promptly to the development and manufacture of new products—the value chain integration we reported on in *Integrated Cost Management* (1993).

Such links are, of course, extraordinarily expensive using traditional methods. CIM, however, is a cost-effective means to obtain the tight cross-functional links demanded by the business strategy. Even though CIM is the lowest-cost tactic that can achieve the business strategy, most managers do not usually view it as a cost-reduction method. Awareness that the communication links are a strategic need is not crystallized enough that it leads to analysis of communication alternatives.

CIM should not be thought of as strategy, but as a low-cost tactic to achieve the strategy of value chain integration. The low-level goal of true CIM installations is to integrate all components of the enterprise into a single, unified system. But CIM must also have the higher goal of improving profitability through value chain integration. The political process surrounding a CIM installation can easily make the CIM system itself appear to be the goal.

Japanese companies have not typically gone all the way to true CIM. However, a survey (FA Report, 1994) revealed that the highest goal was the integration of management with manufacturing and technology (33 percent) followed by the integration of marketing with manufacturing and technology (24 percent), and the integration of technology with manufacturing (24 percent).

Although typical Japanese companies strive to integrate marketing into engineering and production, they sometimes end up integrating management into engineering and production. For example, in NSK, the largest manufacturer of bearings in Japan, a division in Fukushima strove to integrate marketing into engineering and production. The division now produces 10 million bearings monthly with only 350 employees, of which only seven are support staff not directly related to shop-floor production. There is only one cost accountant in the division. What made this thorough rationalization possible was that the overall management was linked and consolidated by a computer network.

Benefits Gained by Introducing CIM

Superior competitiveness in a new market comes from cost, flexibility, quality and service. CIM has an effect on all four of these areas:

A company needs to maintain low *costs* in order to establish a competitive price. Direct labor was reduced through FA, but indirect costs increased greatly. Furthermore, the potential for explosive increases in cost exists when tightening the linkages between functional areas, particularly if using traditional methods. CIM strives not only to reduce direct labor costs, but also to reduce overhead and materials cost through use of innovative software linkages.

Although quantitative evaluation of *flexibility* is difficult, increasing flexibility makes it possible to respond more quickly to market needs and customer desires. Making different products and different amounts at a low cost becomes possible. Products also can be developed rapidly and a company can fit production to the needs of the market.

Quality means maintaining high standards and increasing the reliability of a product. Claims and returns due to product defects will decrease, and the reliability of products will substantially increase due to improvement in quality from installing CIM.

Service, as used here, refers specifically to shortening delivery times and to improving customer service. Focusing on delivery times maintains the rate at which products are delivered—from the time an order for a product is received, developed and designed to the time it is shipped—in order to improve the quality of service to customers. By reducing delivery times, the lead time (the time from when materials are ordered to the time a product emerges) is significantly shortened.

The Impact of CIM on Business Management

The conversion to FA and CIM has five main effects on companies:

1. *Coherent, Integrated System for Management* A coherent, integrated linkage of the company's marketing, engineering and production becomes reasonably possible. Because this linkage reduces the cost of design, testing, and production, companies can design new products more quickly and efficiently.

2. *Organization* In the CIM environment, a company responds to the changing needs of customers and must carry out flexible production.

Marketing must drive manufacturing, and not the other way around. An organization that has adopted a participatory style (Koenig, 1990), such as a network system, is more adaptive. A typical example of Japanese organization is the Syukan (product manager) in Nissan, which is the organization devised for target costing. The Syukan is responsible for a product from its product planing to marketing.

3. *Reduction of Indirect Labor* The introduction of industrial robots eliminates direct labor. Employees directly involved in production are replaced by monitoring, maintenance, R&D, and software development personnel. With CIM, the focus is on reducing planning, design and paperwork. Hence we expect a relative reduction in personnel involved in indirect tasks, the number of which was increased by FA.

4. *Scientific Methods of Analysis* Traditionally, companies had to rely on unscientific methods such as making estimates only on the basis of past experience. As a result of superiority in communication resulting from CIM, management style has become more scientific, and more precise decision-making is possible than in the past.

5. *Increased Impact of Computer Software* Computers, of course, are used more with CIM, so it is no surprise that the use of software increases. The cost of software is so enormous that it will

exceed the cost of tangible assets in the next decade. In fact, for a few very advanced firms today, more than 50 percent of the cost of sales would be allocated software cost—if the accounting standards permitted such allocation. Thus, accounting and cost management for software or information technology will be increasingly important to management, perhaps even becoming the most important single cost component in the near future.

These changes have led to large alterations in the cost-management systems commonly used. In the next chapter we present the basic changes.

III.

THE CHANGE IN COST
MANAGEMENT SYSTEMS
IN THE AGE OF CIM

I N THE PRIOR CHAPTERS we saw how the Japanese business environment has evolved and how the evolution was supported by the five changes in the business culture. Now we will look at the subsequent changes in the cost management systems.

Several new techniques have become important in CIM. The most important is target costing, which, in addition to standard costing, has been used widely by Japanese companies for managing total costs. Two newer arrivals are activity-based costing (ABC), which is used by major U.S. companies to improve overhead allocations, and direct charge of overhead to product line system (DCOPLS), which Japanese companies believe is more effective for cost reduction. Perhaps the greatest impact of CIM has been on the use of standard costing. Budgeting has also become more important, particularly in reducing costs of marketing, R&D and overhead.

Declining Role of Standard Costing in Cost Control

Standard costing has been one of the most used cost control tools in business for several decades. Now, however, the cost control role of standard costing in advanced manufacturing technology (AMT) has declined dramatically, even as its financial statement preparation role has increased in importance. There are three main reasons for the change:

First, the main purpose of standard costing is to raise each worker's efficiency on the shop floor. In AMT such tools are not helpful because industrial robots work at the same level of efficiency at all times.

Second, product diversification and short product life cycles have made setting standard costs extremely difficult. Standard costing, as a practical matter, needs an environment where production costs do not fluctuate often, and where the product itself does not change often.

Finally, the role of cost control at the production and assembly stage has been declining, also as a result of product diversification and shortening of the product life cycle. The focus of cost management has shifted from the production and assembly stages to the planning and design stages.

Cost accountants at Japanese companies such as Toyota, Nissan, NEC and Hitachi unanimously reveal that detailed variance analysis, as conducted more than thirty years ago, is no longer carried out in AMT.

	Historical Costing		Standard Costing	
	number	%	number	%
Traditional Facilities	14	21	9	10
FMS	17	25	15	17
FA	23	51	46	52
CIM	2	3	18	21
Total	67	100	88	100

Figure 5. *The use of standard costing in Japan*

Financial Statement Role
of Standard Costing Increases

In contrast, the use of standard costing to prepare financial statements or improve cost accounting procedures has actually increased in AMT. Moreover, standard costing still plays an important role in mass-produced, process-oriented industries. For example, Matushita Battery, the biggest producer of electric batteries in Japan, uses standard costing as an indispensable tool for cost control.

Increase in the Role of Budgeting

The use of budgeting for cost planning and control has increased considerably. Budgeting not only helps control costs but serves a critical function in planning as well. This definition of budgeting broadens its reach to include direct costs, which have traditionally been controlled by standard costing, and to encompass such indirect costs as marketing, R&D, and factory overhead.

At least three factors contributed to the increased use of budgeting:

First, the increase in indirect costs due to FA—indirect labor such as design, maintenance, supervisory services, R&D, and software development—has increased. Budgeting is an effective tool for managing each of these costs.

Second, the importance of cost planning and control have increased at the upstream stages (R&D, planning and design) and final downstream stages (sales promotion, physical distribution). Budgeting is also effective for managing these upstream and downstream costs. That is, cost management has become more strategic.

Last, those managers who face technological innovation in diversified operations or in group management need effective management systems. These systems have become very important for profit planning in Japan.

	number	%
No Budget	5	3
Only Profit Planning	22	14
Profit Planning as Budgeting	21	13
Profit Planning and Budgeting	109	69
No Answer	1	1
Total	158	100

Figure 6.   The use of budgeting in Japan
Adapted from: Sakurai, Michiharu, and Paul Scarbrough, Integrated Cost Management, *Productivity Press 1995. Used with permission.*

In the United States, profit planning is part of budgeting. This is not true in Japan, where only 13 percent of the respondents have this form of budgeting. Generally speaking, only companies with a top-down style of management seem to use this approach.

New Techniques of Cost Management

In addition to the changes in the traditional techniques of standard costing and budgeting, several new tools have arisen from the push to AMT. Primarily to manage direct costs, target costing has been widely used by Japanese companies and it supplements standard costing. Catch-ball budgeting is the most popular type of budgeting in Japanese companies. It separates profit planning from budgeting and then joins them late in the process. For managing indirect costs, activity-based costing (ABC) has been proposed and used in some major U.S. companies. In Japanese companies, however, a different system has also been developed, which can be called direct charge of overhead to product line system (DCOPLS).

Wide Use of Target Costing

Product diversification, life cycle shortening, and widespread use of industrial robots have made "make-to-cost" increasingly important at the planning and design stages. Target costing (TC) is a multidisciplinary tool of cost management to reduce overall costs applied at the planning and design stages with cooperation of the engineering, production, marketing, development and accounting departments. TC is discussed extensively in a separate chapter.

CIM and TC are mutually reinforcing. First, CIM expedites the use of TC because it can reduce costs at the planning and design stages, which is where CIM operates most intensively. Second, the cooperation of the marketing, engineering and production departments, with the accounting department as coordinator, becomes critical for the successful operation of target costing. Since CIM itself demands the cooperation of marketing, engineering, and production, the two techniques tend to reinforce each other.

Budgeting As Catch

Profit planning for short-range business and strategic purposes begins at the executive level, using a top-down approach. It reflects the strategic profit needs of the organization for ensuring survival and growth of the firm and its affiliates. Then departmental budgets are prepared using a bottom-up approach with the profit plan as a target. If there is a gap in target profit between the profit plan and the budget (which there usually is), the process continues until there is no gap or both sides agree that it is not possible to close the gap (which happens occasionally). A company's prosperity depends on playing this kind of "catch" between top management and managers at the operational level. It is sometimes called "catch ball" budgeting. This type of budgeting is the main source of kaizen ideas in most companies.

ABC and DCOPLS

Those companies with CIM find it crucial in effectively managing overhead costs. This applies across industries, since overhead has increased both as a proportion of total cost and in total. The increasing overhead costs include engineering support, maintenance, planning and design, setup, material handling and quality inspection. Unfortunately, current accounting practice does not provide good solutions for managing overhead effectively.

Current Major Japanese Practices of Overhead Allocation. Most Japanese academies and practitioners believe that they can manage overhead through budgetary control with the help of middle-range business planning. For management and control purposes, Japanese cost accountants have vigorously sought more reasonable allocation bases, especially since the installation of FMS began. For preparing financial statements, of course, a company cannot avoid allocating overhead, even if it involves arbitrary computation.

Activity-Based Costing (ABC). The original ABC allocates overhead using more sophisticated allocation bases, known as cost drivers, and therefore supplies better information for strategic cost analysis and cost control. This form of ABC was dominant mainly from the 1980s to 1991, and focused principally on accurate overhead allocation.

Direct Charge of Overhead to Product Line System (DCOPLS). Japanese managers focus more interest on reducing costs rather than on allocating overhead, which does not contribute to cost reduction. To reduce costs, they should be directly charged to a product or products, not be allocated. Quite a few Japanese companies have

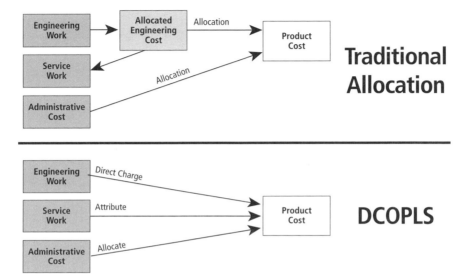

Figure 7. DCOPLS and traditional allocation

selected the product line instead of the product as the cost object. They constructed cost accounting systems with few allocations, which are thus useful for cost reduction, but not for accurate product costing. The DCOPLS, with its focus on cost reduction, stands in sharp contrast to the original ABC, with its focus on product cost and its lack of a process view.

However, this does not mean that Japanese managers ignore accurate allocations through activities. In fact, many companies allocate overhead through activity-related multiple rates. Others charge overhead to the product line for reducing costs effectively.

Historical Costing	Departmental Costing	26%
	Process Costing	7%
	Job-order Costing	44%
Standard Costing	Process Costing	3%
	Job-order Costing	10%
Variable Costing	Process Costing	1%
	Job-order Costing	5%
Standard Variable Costing	Process	1%
	Job-order Costing	3%

Figure 8. *Cost accounting systems of a software factory*
Adapted from: Sakurai, Michiharu, and Paul Scarbrough, Integrated
Cost Management, *Productivity Press 1995. Used with permission.*

Management for Software Development and Information Processing Costs

The amount of computer software used in business increases year by year as the use of computers increases. As a natural consequence, cost management for software has become one of the essential management issues in Japanese companies. We discuss this topic at length in a separate chapter.

We note that cost accounting for software has developed as CIM develops. Generally, *at least* 40 percent of FA facility costs come from software. If companies install

CIM, computer use will increase dramatically and, of course, software use will also increase. Thus, it seems appropriate for companies to install cost accounting systems as automation proceeds.

Cost accounting for software allows software developers to control software development costs effectively. Charge-back systems give effective control over use of hardware and software to evaluate employee or department performance in using information processing services. Companies will have to improve existing systems to cope with the rise in software development costs and information processing costs.

Conclusion

Japanese firms have a strong tendency toward cost management. In several instances—for example DCOPLS—they use techniques that they know to be less-precise measures of product cost in order to direct the behavior of employees toward certain goals. Thus, the cost accounting system binds itself more tightly to the strategic mission and less tightly to concerns about precision in measurement than in the United States.

Where Does This Lead?

The FA/CIM environment has led to the dominance of several accounting techniques, most importantly, target costing. In the next chapter we take a look at target costing and how it works.

IV.

TARGET COSTING FOR
STRATEGIC COST MANAGEMENT

ARGET COSTING IS THE MOST important new
Japanese cost management tool. It is used as the
main tool of innovation in the IKM management
doctrine. As we described earlier, most management
efforts in Japan focus on the three themes of innovation,
kaizen (continuous improvement) and maintenance.
Overlaid on this management focus, the framework for
cost management uses the following: target costing for
innovation, kaizen costing for kaizen and cost maintenance for maintaining cost at historical levels.

Target costing comprehensively manages cost by
focusing on a total life cycle cost reduction through innovation in design and production. To reduce costs it integrates production and marketing functions, with engineering as the core discipline. Independently, the CIM environment integrates the production, technology and marketing functions with a communications network to
improve their interaction. Since CIM and target costing
both involve a similar integration, most companies use

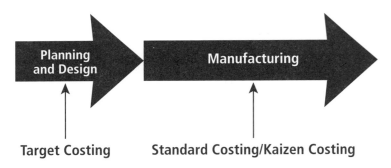

Figure 9. The relationship between
target costing and kaizen costing
Adapted from: Sakurai, Michiharu, and Paul Scarbrough, Integrated
Cost Management, *Productivity Press 1995. Use with permission.*

them together. Using target cost in conjunction with a
CIM environment enhances communications and thus
makes both more powerful. In fact, we can reasonably
view CIM as contributing to corporate effectiveness
mainly by providing the communications support for
target costing.

Kaizen costing involves both cost-reduction activities
for each product and cost-reduction activities for each cost.
Generally, companies control direct material and direct
labor costs through VE and other engineering activities.
In contrast, they manage overhead mainly through budgeting and the use of the wisdom and know-how of all
employees, using TQC, TPM and other techniques.

Maintaining costs was very important in the past. In
the CIM environment, however, its importance has dimin-
ished remarkably because industrial robots can produce
quality products with low cost. Cost maintenance means
setting price and quantity standards for product costs and

then ensuring that actual results closely match the standards. For the new product, cost maintenance means attaining target costs set by target costing. In the existing product, standard costing plays a role in reaching and stabilizing operations at the standard cost. Cost-maintenance activities consist of cost-control activities undertaken to control departmental costs, productivity, unit price and equipment.

Definition and Purpose of Target Costing

Although no universally recognized definition for target costing exists, generically it has three main components:

1. A target cost is set for a product based on the company's strategic policy.

2. Design-to-cost responsibility is then assigned to cross-functional teams with extremely broad authority. This authority includes, of course, product features, and can also extend to all upstream and downstream support activities and their method of delivery.

3. Cost-reduction activity continues until the target cost is achieved or all parties realize it is not possible.

It is important to keep in mind, however, that the technique itself is not as important as the manner of its use. In Japan, this system resides in the network of relationships created by the seven business innovations described earlier. That is, the target costing technique is implemented by people with several important characteristics:

1. They work better in groups.

2. They have a more complete perspective of the value chain due to job rotations.

3. They are personally committed to innovation, kaizen and maintenance.

On the market side, the spread of target costing in Japan is driven by the shortening of product life cycles and intensification of international competition. If products have to be designed and redesigned more frequently, then cost-reduction efforts must focus on the design process. On the internal side, the spread of target costing is driven by the move from traditional production to FA and then to CIM. This move has put in place the integrated communication structures between engineering, production and marketing that are needed to support target costing.

The operational push toward target costing is now seen as a tool for strategic cost management. Since the late 1980s target costing has become even more closely connected with business strategy and thus a strategic cost-management tool for attaining the target profit specified by middle-range business planning. For example, Nissan sets target cost based on target profit which, in turn, is based on business strategy and customer needs. Thus, target costing should now be considered a strategic cost management tool for profit planning as well as cost reduction.

With the aid of hindsight, we see that, when used most effectively, the general purposes of target costing are:

1. Strategic cost reduction—reducing *total* costs, including manufacturing, marketing, and user's costs, while maintaining high quality.

2. Strategic profit planning—formulating strategic profit plans by integrating marketing information with engineering and production factors.

Characteristics of Target Costing

1. Target costing is used in the *planning and design stages* as shown in Figure 9.

2. Target costing is a tool for *cost reduction.* Conceptually, cost management can be divided into two parts: cost reduction (or cost planning) and cost control. Target costing is clearly focused on cost reduction.

3. Target costing is a *market-driven* technique.

4. Target costing is usually part of *strategic* profit planning for multiple years. In fact, target costing is often used as a bottom-up tool for attaining the profit goal set by top management when it determines middle-range corporate strategy. Thus, the cost-reduction program is more strategic than operational.

5. Target costing is an *engineering-oriented* technique. Target costing is a management tool for directing and focusing the decision process for design specifications and production engineering.

Financial accounting measurements are not emphasized, and the method has more of a management engineering characteristic. Hence, it coincides with other Japanese management engineering techniques such as VE, TQC and JIT.

6. Target costing depends on and enforces extremely high levels of *cooperation* between departments. In target costing, the accounting department acts as the coordinator and information provider while the marketing, engineering (planning and design) and production departments determine success or failure. It is at this point that we find the convergence of target costing and CIM, which also integrates marketing, engineering and production.

Target Costing in Manufacturing Companies

Target costing has three main conceptual steps:

1. New product planning focusing on customer satisfaction

2. Determining a target cost through company strategic policy and aligning it with achievable costs

3. Attaining target cost by using VE and other cost-reduction techniques

The allowable cost is calculated by subtracting the target profit from the planned sales price. The allowable cost is known as the "maximum permissible manufacturing cost." It is the desired cost based only on market conditions. The next step is to figure out if the product can be made for this amount. So the "drifting cost" is calculated for each part based on accounting records. This drifting cost is also referred to as an estimated or base cost and is a current estimated cumulative cost, with no target in mind. It is called the drifting cost because it is continuously recalculated as the VE work is performed. The primary work in target costing is, in fact, the VE effort to reduce the drifting cost to equal the allowable cost. The cost reductions come from both the usual discovery of better methods and, most importantly, from trading off costs across functional boundaries (for example, increasing costs in one department to gain cost reductions in another).

The index used in setting the target profit is usually the return on sales (ROS) rather than the return on investment (ROI). One of the reasons for using ROS is the ease of calculating the ROS for each product. But the most important reason is that the use of ROS is strategically superior to ROI as will be discussed in Chapter 6.

The target cost is usually only attained through a painstaking VE program. If the drifting cost does not reach the strived-for goal, then additional cost-reduction activities are carried out with VE programs for second, and third estimates. Finally an attainable target cost is established that can be the goal for production efforts.

After a settling-in period, a report on performance is examined to check whether any cost standards have not been achieved. If any abnormalities have occurred, kaizen costing committees bring out the problems for discussion, and to propose further improvement. Thus, target costing is also a cost-reduction activity based on self-imposed improvement efforts by the factory. An indispensable condition leading to its success is that each employee should participate in the cost-reduction activity. A significant drawback is that it can be too stressful on the employees. A number of companies are reassessing how they manage the target-costing process in order to lessen the adverse impacts on employees. The reasonableness of the target will determine the reactions of the employees.

Method of Setting Target Cost

The target is tied to the strategic policy of the company. In setting the target cost, there are many links with management accounting. The combination method, which is the method presented above as the example of target costing, is a method consolidating the operating focus on profitability and the technological focus on feasibility.

The main approach practiced in Japanese companies is the combination of top-down target cost goals and bottom-up responses presented above. More than half (57 percent) of the Japanese companies we surveyed (106 companies listed on the Tokyo Stock Exchange) used the combination method. The case presented in this book is based on the combination method.

Cost Tables and VE

Companies using target costing find cost tables helpful. The cost table is a tool for estimating such costs as

materials, parts, utility, conversion and other costs easily
and accurately. There are several kinds of cost tables: one
for effectively purchasing parts and material, one for evaluating performance, and one for defining manufacturing
methods and their corresponding costs. There are also
both detailed and rough cost tables.

Unlike standard cost cards, cost tables are focused
not only on parts or products, but also on activities. They
include time and cost estimates for most of the activities
that a machine could perform. Having these tables enables
engineers to rapidly estimate the cost of alternative
designs. In fact, it is akin to having an activity-based data
set for potential activities as well as for current activities.

Originally, cost tables were developed and used to
estimate the price of purchased parts, but they are now
used as a tool for accurately estimating production costs
and profit on purchased parts. They are also used as data
for showing in-house manufacturing costs. For example,
Nippondenso, the top producer of electronic and electrical
parts in Japan, uses cost tables as a tool for setting standard costs by estimating such factors as material requirements, conversion processes, plant and equipment, labor
hours and conversion cost rate in an orderly method.

Many Japanese companies computerize cost tables to
make them more efficient and sophisticated. For example,
Nippondenso has 22 types of cost tables in its computer
system.

In Japan the cost reduction in target costing is performed by VE. VE is similar to VA (value analysis) used
in the United States, but different in several aspects. VE
is a method for doing systematic research on each function

of a product or service to learn how to attain required functions at the lowest total cost. In other words, it is a method or tool for re-engineering the functions or purposes of a product or service for the purpose of improving the quality or value in order to get customer satisfaction with the lowest cost.

VE can be applied to manufacturing and to service industries. In target costing, VE is one of the keys to effective new product development.

VE proposals consist of both idea proposals and action proposals. Improvement efforts usually focus on manufacturing, but other areas also have room for cost reduction.

For example, the cash savings from VE improvements in one electronics company in fiscal year 1991 revealed that 70 percent came from manufacturing, 12 percent from marketing costs, 9 percent from design, 5 percent form clerical activities, and 4 percent from software and other areas. In Japanese companies, specialists do not have a monopoly on VE. Normally, people conduct the VE analysis concurrently with their normally assigned job. Most companies consider idea proposals an important part of innovation and kaizen, and bonuses are commonly paid as compensation for the proposals.

To make target costing most successful, target costing must be conducted for each product with a matrix organization linking each of the departments: planning, designing, accounting, production, and marketing. For example, Company Z (an automobile manufacturer) introduced target costing several years ago but could not make it work successfully. Later is changed organizational structure and made the powerful product manager responsible for target costing. This change strongly emphasized the importance of target costing and rescued the company's program.

Integration of Middle-range Business Planning into Target Costing

Middle-range business planning, another new device, ties in with CIM and target costing. Companies currently believe they should have middle-range business planning, and that it should closely coordinate with corporate strategy. Japanese managers realized that long-range business planning was unsuitable in a changing business environ-

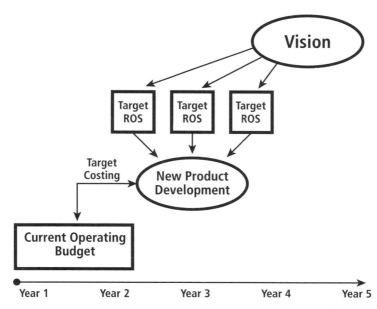

Figure 10.   Middle-range planning and target costing

ment because since the oil crisis of 1973, no one has been able to predict successfully very far ahead. Nowadays, typical Japanese companies use middle-range business planning accompanied by a long-range vision. They do not use long-range business planning.

Middle-range business planning provides the best business venue for new product planning, and target costing provides the essential mechanism for integrating business strategy into these plans.

Some studies report almost 70 percent of the responding Japanese managers integrate middle-range business planning into target costing.

The middle-range business planning horizon typically extends for three years. One of the most important parts is the new product development projects, which are prepared by the engineering or development department. The business planning department, an upper-management staff department, coordinates the project plans, including the new product-development projects, and integrates them into a formal middle-range business plan. The department head of the target costing department usually discusses new products with engineering managers well in advance, so that the target costing manager typically supports the project, which is originally prepared by the engineering department.

Case Study on Target Costing

How is the target cost set? How do companies conduct the analysis for target cost? In order to illustrate the process of determining and analyzing target cost, we will present a target cost example from Company X.

Determination of Target Cost

Company X plans to develop a new automobile, the Crusader. As shown in Figure 11, the product development plan is created by a new product development committee. Management designates a project team and sets a cost target. The team consists of several specialists from different departments such as engineering, marketing, purchasing and accounting.

The Product Development Committee decided to produce an automobile that will sell at a planned sales price of 4 million yen. The target profit was determined using the ROS imbedded in corporate strategy of 20 percent. At 20 percent of 4 million yen, the target profit was 800,000 yen. Subtracting the target profit of 800,000 yen

Steps	Cost Reduction Program	Committees
Development	Discussion of Customer Needs	Product Develoment Committee
Planning	Estimating Target Cost	Product Design Committee
Conceptual Design	Team Activities	Zero Target Cost Committee
Product Design	VE	
Trial Production	VE	1st Target Cost Committee
Appraisal of Test	VE	
Final Test	VE	2nd Target Cost Committee
First Production	Set Standards	3rd Target Cost Committee
Mass Production	Kaizen Costing	Production Committee

Figure 11. Target cost administration
Adapted from: Sakurai, Michiharu, and Paul Scarbrough, Integrated Cost Management, Productivity Press 1995. Used with permission.

from the planned sales price of 4 million yen yielded an allowable cost of 3.2 million yen. The target cost teams were formed and their activities began.

Engineers pulled together the drifting cost based on present technological standards. The drifting cost was 3.5 million yen. This was 300,000 yen more than the allowable cost. VE projects were conducted several times for cost reduction. The results were presented to the first Target Costing Committee, and the plan was studied further to find more room for cost reduction. Target cost was tentatively established as 3.2 million yen.

The cost was reduced by 30,000 yen in upholstery, 2,000 in the drive shaft, 10,000 in the engine, 40,000 in direct conversion costs, and so on. Finally, they were able to reduce costs down to 3.225 million yen. These results were presented to the second Target Costing Committee. They could not eliminate another 25,000 yen of costs to come down to the allowable cost without changing the desired product functions.

The third Target Costing Committee decided that 3.2 million yen would have to be the target cost, and that it would be necessary to focus on cost-control activities during the manufacturing process to eliminate the 25,000 yen variance. This resulted in 3.2 million yen being firmly established as the target cost for the new model automobile. This target cost was considered the standard cost and the company placed its hopes on cost control in the manufacturing stage.

Analysis of Target Cost

All preparation for mass-production was finished and production of the Crusader began. Fortunately, cost-reduction activities through VE before manufacturing were satisfactory. That is, cost reductions to 3.2 million yen were made by this stage.

The new product, the Crusader, was very popular. However, an economic downturn caused production volume to fall. Sales volume was originally projected at 20,000 cars, however, only 18,000 cars were sold.

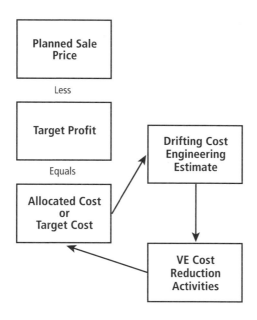

Figure 12. Determining target cost
Adapted from: Sakurai, Michiharu, and Paul Scarbrough, Integrated
Cost Management, *Productivity Press 1995. Used with permission.*

Nevertheless, in light of the economy, the Crusader did well.

One month after the beginning of production, actual results were accumulated and variance analysis against the target cost was conducted.

The variance analysis led to two findings: First, because of favorable material and parts costs, total material costs were reduced by 40,000 yen per car. The result of other cost reduction efforts was 10,000 yen per car. Second, because of the decrease in sales volume, fixed cost per unit increased by 60,000 yen per car. As a result, the actual result was over target cost by 10,000 yen per car. That is, actual cost was 3.21 million yen.

At the third Target Costing Committee, a discussion was focused on how to reduce the actual cost to the 3.2 million yen target cost per car. As a result of the discussion, a proposal was submitted to rotate 300 production people to the sales department for a sales promotion. This made sense only because of the experience of the staff in prior job rotations in the firm. Executives and workers of Company X agreed to this project the next month.

Cost Management for Software

Target costing should not be considered a method peculiar to controlling costs of hardware. It also should be seen as a useful method for managing costs of computer software. The main reason for this is the importance of cost reduction in the planning and design stages of software development.

Figure 13. Cost management for software
Adapted from: Sakurai, Michiharu, and Paul Scarbrough, Integrated
Cost Management, *Productivity Press 1995. Used with permission.*

One of the successful software applications of target costing was reported by NEC. Target costing for software is conceptually the same as for hardware but it uses different methods. The structure of target costing in NEC is depicted in Figure 13.

Conclusion

Target costing is a tool for strategic cost management developed originally in Japan and focused primarily on the assembly-oriented industries. It is rapidly spreading to the process-oriented industries, software manufacturers, and other industries. Target costing is a process that is most effective in the high-technology environments of CIM. Nonetheless, this is not to say that there are no problems with this technique. Regardless of how skillfully one introduces target costing, if each and every employee does not actively try to reduce costs, it will have no effect. Also, target costing can easily make unreasonable demands on the workplace.

Target costing works in Japan because the people and administrative structure respond to the needs of the method. Without the business culture of this kind, we are likely to get something that looks like target costing, but which is not very effective. For example, a division of General Motors attempted to use target costing in the late 1980s only to meet total and complete failure when the engineering department withdrew all participation in mid-process. Why? Assigning cost reduction targets to subcomponents is an intense and political process in Japan, which relies on the experience and judgment of mid-level and senior managers, all of whom have similar backgrounds and experience because of job rotations. GM, on the other hand, attempted to use the statistical analysis of a survey to assign subtargets. These subtargets were not considered realistic or rational by engineering. In fact, the method assigned the responsibility for the largest cost reduction to the auto frame design group because customer surveys showed that customers did not consider the frame important. When engineering could not convince management of the folly of the assignment, they stopped participating and the project collapsed with a loss of several million dollars.

V.

INVESTMENT JUSTIFICATION
IN CIM

T HE TYPICAL JAPANESE APPROACH to investment justification differs from what we usually see in the
United States. Traditionally, discussion focused
on the superiority of either the internal rate of return
(IRR) method or net present value (NPV) method, with
passing reference to the payback method. However, for
FA and CIM investments, other issues require attention
because investment for automation does not simply reduce
labor input. Many indirect and intangible benefits that are
difficult to quantify result from such an investment, and
we should regard an analysis as complete only when it
takes them into consideration. The techniques discussed
in this chapter need the support of the seven business
innovations identified earlier. In particular, the use of
cross-functional teams composed of people with very
broad backgrounds gives the intellectual power needed
to address this difficult issue.

Before we explain the nature of the decision methods,
we need to define clearly the differences between traditional investment and investment in automated equipment.

The Difference between Traditional and Automated Equipment

Purpose

Investment in traditional equipment and facilities aims to increase productivity by reducing labor costs and by conserving energy. However, automated equipment provides value in many ways other than reducing labor input. These purposes include improving quality, reducing inventories, reducing floor space, and reducing the need to perform dangerous tasks.

Capability

Traditional equipment is comparatively limited in use. Automated equipment has more uses, but requires a much higher level of skill to take full advantage of its capabilities. It also involves a large number of unknowns, and most companies have limited experience in dealing with automated equipment. The success of investing in CIM and creative use of its software depends largely on the ability to gather information needed for effective use of the equipment.

Intangible Benefits

The large number of indirect and intangible benefits associated with automated equipment make it much more difficult to estimate the impact on profits. While one can readily calculate the results of reducing labor costs, scheduling, set-up time, and reducing work-in-process inventory, the following are very difficult to estimate:

1. The benefits derived from improvements in quality, reduction in delivery time, increased flexibility and competitive advantage

2. Future operating costs of automated equipment

3. The cost of CIM information systems

4. The economic life of equipment

5. The potential loss in sales from failing to automate

Cooperative Work

Unlike investments in traditional equipment, investments in automated equipment and CIM have strategic implications. Thus, investments in automated equipment and CIM should involve more people throughout the organization than investment in traditional equipment. Consequently, communication among the various fields of operations, manufacturing, engineering, information systems, production management and accounting is essential. Here, then, is one of the strong ties to the seven business innovations and to target costing. The cooperative work approach needed in CIM is supported by the other facets of the business culture.

Mini-Investment

Investment in CIM is an endless project. Instead of scale, economies of scope must be attained in CIM investment. However, the investment is likely to be big because of the cost of using cutting-edge technologies.

Given these differences between the two types of investment, computing the relevant benefits and costs will be extremely difficult. In the next section we will discuss the problems thoroughly.

Forecasting the Profits and Costs Related to Automation

The factors that are important to consider when investing in equipment differ depending on the degree of automation. Howell and Soucy (1987) classified the degree of automation into level 1 (traditional equipment), level 2 (FMS), and level 3 (CIM). The corresponding factors for each level are shown in Figure 14. As the level of automation increases, the intangible benefits become more important.

As indicated in Figure 14, level 2 equipment such as numerical control (NC) machines, unmanned transport systems and unmanned warehouses requires investments in software. Level 3 investments require building and maintaining information systems for networks and databases.

The direct benefits of levels 2 and 3 are comparable. However, compared to traditional equipment, there are significant benefits in both quality improvement and inventory reduction.

Under FMS, support functions such as design, maintenance, monitoring, production planning, R&D and software development must be beefed up. However, moving to level 3 will decrease requirements for support staff due to automated design, automated maintenance and other

Description	Level 1 (Traditional)	Level 2 (FMS)	Level 3 (CIM)
Object	Plant and Equipment	Plant and Equipment Software	Plant and Equipment Software Network
Direct Profit	Labor Reduction Energy Savings	Labor Reduction Energy Conservation Scrap Decrease Inventory Reduction	Labor Reduction Energy Conservation Scrap Decrease Inventory Reduction
Indirect Profit	Danger Reduction	Danger Reduction Support Increase Space Reduction	Danger Reduction Support Increase Space Reduction Lead Time
Benefit		Quality Flexibility	Quality Flexibility Service to Customer Competitiveness Throughput Learning Effect

Figure 14. Benefits gained from automation
Adapted from: Sakurai, Michiharu, and Paul Scarbrough, **Integrated**
Cost Management, *Productivity Press 1995. Used with permission.*

factors. It will also be possible to shorten lead time due
to CIM integration of the engineering and production systems with sales. Being able to respond to customers more
rapidly improves the company's competitive position and
is likely to result in more throughput. Considering the
learning effect, conversion to CIM is an indispensable
requirement for the next phase of automation, just as FA
was the prerequisite for CIM.

Costs are easier to quantify than revenues. Figure
15 lists some costs of CIM equipment and facilities. The
easier-to-quantify costs include depreciation, interest, labor
costs, costs for utilities (electricity and gas, etc.) and instal-

Quantifiable Costs	Unquantifiable Costs
Cash Flow of Plant and Equipment Capital Costs for Plant and Equipment Labor Costs Utilities Maintenance Costs Software Costs Others	In-house Training Costs Costs for System Operation Infrastructure Others

Figure 15. Cost estimate for CIM
Adapted from: Sakurai, Michiharu, and Paul Scarbrough, Integrated Cost Management, Productivity Press 1995. Used with permission.

lation. More difficult to quantify are company training costs and system management costs.

The Benefits of Investing in CIM

Reduction in Labor Costs and Energy Conservation

Although direct labor costs decrease with the introduction of FMS equipment, support costs such as maintenance, monitoring, product planning, design, R&D, and software development increase significantly. As a company advances to FA from FMS, the need for design personnel decreases because of the application of CAD. The introduction of CIM links engineering and production with marketing and aims for operations that can quickly adopt environmental changes. Its focus is on reducing indirect labor costs and reducing cycle time.

As automation increases, equipment becomes smaller in scale and more efficient. As a result, energy can be conserved.

Reduction in Inventories

It is possible to reduce work-in-process and finished goods inventories significantly with automated equipment. This is accomplished by increasing flexibility in the production schedule, creating an orderly flow of goods, increasing quality and improving schedule management. There is also a tax benefit from reducing inventories.

Quality Improvement

One of the major effects that can be expected, along with a reduction in direct labor costs, is improvement in quality. Robots can perform simple tasks with a great deal of precision and reliability, which reduces need for testing facilities and personnel.

Reduction in Floor Space

Compared to traditional equipment and facilities, those that are automated tend to be smaller in size and number because of greater flexibility and sophistication. As a result, floor space and warehouse space can be reduced.

Shorter Lead Time and Throughput

CIM integrates production and engineering with marketing and therefore can drastically cut lead time. For example, Yamazaki Steel shortened the mean processing time for one unit from 35 days to a day and a half. Part of the benefit of reducing the lead time is smaller inventories—which has already been considered above.

Increased Flexibility

Because product specifications can be changed easily, one can change a product to conform with the needs of the customers. This is often practiced in automated automobile factories, where the products coming down the assembly line differ from each other. In short, one of the advantages of using automated equipment and facilities is that simple changes in the flow may be made with ease.

Reduction in Dangerous Operations

The introduction of FA has decreased the number of dangerous and physically taxing operations performed by people, which has cut the occurrence of industrial accidents.

Recruiting the Work Force

Recruiting and retaining the manufacturing work force has become a major problem in Japan. For example, today the best graduates from Tokyo University tend to work for banks or insurance companies rather than for manufacturing companies, which have a dirty image.

The Learning Effect and Competitive Advantage

Investments in new technologies have an important learning effect. Thus, even if the direct cash flows associated with a particular investment are negative, the investment may sometimes be indispensable just to maintain knowledge and hence future competitiveness.

Considering the rapid pace of technological innovation, companies that put off capital investments until new markets develop have no future. Moreover, if a company has not mastered a given level of automation, it cannot go on to the next level and will be left behind by the competition. Companies that did not have any experience with FMS were not able to install FA successfully.

Investment in CIM increases the company's ability to compete on a multidimensional rather than a unidimensional basis. Companies are simultaneously in a position to offer high-quality product at low cost and provide fast and flexible product changes. A number of authors have identified the ability to compete on multiple bases as a key strategic imperative.

Choosing a Method of Investment Justification

The DCF Method and U.S. Companies

DCF methods, and in particular the internal rate of return (IRR), are the most popular methods of evaluating investments in the United States. The net present value (NPV) method is also a very popular method among U.S. accountants for automated equipment as well. The payback method was used more frequently when evaluating investments in automated equipment than when evaluating investments in traditional investment. However, the payback method is frequently criticized because "it does not consider all the project's cash flows or the time value of money, so its use could cause the company to make bad investment decisions" (Band & Hendricks, 1987). It is generally agreed that the IRR and the NPV methods are superior to the payback method for evaluating investments in CIM equipment (Polakoff, 1990).

The Overall Evaluation and Payback in Japanese Companies

Japanese companies do not normally justify investment solely on the basis of economic factors and take other quantitative and nonquantitative factors into account.

Since many factors in investing in CIM cannot be quantified, an overall evaluation that incorporates strategic considerations is superior to an analysis based solely on quantifiable economic factors. With CIM, such intangible benefits as flexibility, improvement in quality, competitive advantage and the learning effect can be of overriding importance.

When Japanese companies use a quantifiable method, they most often use the payback method. Mr. Koike, the statutory auditor of NEC, commented that a two-year payback period is appropriate for his company. With NEC, the payback method is used not because it is simple but because the goal is a quick recovery of capital. This raises an interesting question. Japanese managers are believed to have a long-term perspective (Kagono et al., 1985), but they use the payback method, which seems to be based on short-term considerations. There are three important issues that influence this:

1. The life cycle of products has been shortening. The average life of a product in Japan is now two to three years. Thus, capital investment must be recovered quickly.

2. The life cycle of equipment has also been getting shorter.

3. Sales of high technology products cannot be accurately predicted. Semiconductors are a typical product of this type. Thus, early recovery of invested capital is *essential*.

An Illustration of Investment Justification

How are investments in CIM actually justified in major Japanese companies? It is difficult to select typical examples because procedures are different depending on the type of business. In the following, we will present an example of the investment in CIM by hypothetical Company X, creating a composite by combining examples from the actual experience of several Japanese companies.

The Process of Decision-Making in Investment Justification

Decisions for investing in CIM equipment involve four stages. First, proposals are generated by relevant departments in the middle-range business planning stage. Next, the framework for investment in plant and equipment is formulated in the policymaking process for budgeting. In the third stage, coordination between executive board and production planning group are made through the budgeting process. Finally, decisions are made about the investments.

Middle-range business plans extend over a two- or three-year period and are rolled forward each year. Within this plan, policies for expansion of operations, proposals for improvement and other important issues are examined every year.

In the first stage, a basic policy is determined, and studies concerning specific numbers are given secondary consideration. What is essential is to determine what action is to be taken. Policymaking is more important than concrete numbers.

In the second stage, an investment proposal is initiated and studied from a company-wide perspective.

In the third stage, a budget proposal is presented in the framework of profit planning. The need for and adequacy of the proposal in CIM equipment is reviewed in relation to the overall investment plan in the production department. Here, a method of economic justification such as payback, ROI or IRR is applied.

In the final stage, after the budget has been determined, a Ringisyo (formal proposal for top management approval) is submitted and final approval of top management is obtained.

What receives approval in addition to the budget proposal are the research report on the investment proposal and the proposal for investment criteria.

The research report on the investment proposal indicates:

- The specifications

- An outline (product, quantity to be produced, process, operating time and period of use)

- The reason for purchase (expansion, conservation of energy, rationalization of operations, reduction in manpower, improvement in quality, reduction in environmental pollution, improvement in operations, renovation and others)

- The conditions for purchase (from another vendor, import, specially ordered, valuation of similar item and others)

- The conditions for purchasing a substitute item

- The evaluation process concerning why a specific vendor was selected

- The results

- The cost-effectiveness

- The future prospects

CIM Investment Criteria

Company X uses a two-stage process to screen projects. In the first stage, investments are evaluated based on their projected payback and profitability. In the second stage, intangible benefits are considered. The primary criteria are shown in Figure 16. The number in the lower line in each block is the weight given to that item.

The secondary criteria are shown in Figure 17. These criteria include effects of the investment on quality, flexibility and competitiveness.

In the overall determination, investment proposals that exceed a score of 30 in the primary criteria and 75 in the secondary criteria tend to be selected. Nonetheless, these are not automatically selected, and ultimately the

Description	Scores					
Profitability Weight	20–30% 30	15–20% 25	10–15% 20	5–10% 10	0–5% 5	Negative 0
Payback (years) Weight	1–2 30		2–4 20		4–6 5	Over 7 0

Figure 16. **The main criteria for investment**
justification in CIM
Adapted from: Sakurai, Michiharu, and Paul Scarbrough, Integrated
Cost Management, *Productivity Press 1995. Used with permission.*

person making the decision, the company president, the executive in charge, or the department head will decide on the basis of corporate strategy. Company X has factories in areas A, B and C. In area A, they produce semiconductors, so that the role of strategic factors is considerable in investment decision. Technological innovation occurs rapidly, product life-cycle is very short, and long-term predictions are difficult. Therefore, in the primary criteria much greater weight is given to payback because early recovery of investment is indispensable for this industry. However, because of the size and strategic nature of this investment, the intangible benefits and the judgment of the company president are likely to prove critical.

On the other hand, area B makes products in which there is hardly any room for technological innovation. Therefore, much greater weight is given to profitability evaluations and the intangible benefits are far fewer.

In area C, the life-cycle of products is short. Consequently, in area C the payback period is set to two years and investments with a payback in excess of two years will be turned down even though the ROI may be satisfactory.

Description	Scores				
Future Outlook	Development 30	Growth 25	Mature 15	Saturation 10	Downward 5
Quality		Greatly 25	High 15	Moderately 10	
Urgency		Essential 25		Important 10	Convenient 5
Flexibility		High 20	Middle 15	Low 10	A Little 5
Delivery			Very Good 15	Good 10	Fair 5
Competitiveness			Very High 15	Strong 10	Fair 5

Figure 17. **Secondary criteria in CIM**
Adapted from: Sakurai, Michiharu, and Paul Scarbrough, **Integrated Cost Management,** *Productivity Press 1995. Used with permission.*

Conclusion

Two important factors bear repeating:

- Although it may be called investment in equipment, investments in CIM also involve enormous investment in software.

- Many of the benefits of CIM are indirect and intangible.

With traditional equipment, it is often sufficient to evaluate investment only by quantifying the profits achieved by reducing manpower and converting the profits each year to present values. However, when evaluating investment in CIM, one must take into account not only profits realized from reductions in manpower, but also indirect and intangible benefits realized from such factors as improvements in quality, reduction in inventories, shortening of lead time, flexibility, competitiveness and others. However, it is very difficult for business managers to include such intangible benefits in the calculations. Ultimately, it is important for top management to make a final decision based on corporate strategy. Companies with effective target costing and CIM have better potential for good investment decisions due to the increased complexity and sophistication of the employee knowledge base.

VI.

COST MANAGEMENT
FOR SOFTWARE

COSTS FOR SOFTWARE ARE a central business issue because successfully using robots and other machines requires superior software. Japan's manufacturing industries are highly developed and can produce quality products at low cost. Japan used approximately 62 percent of the world's robots as early as 1992 (Japan Industrial Robots Industry Association).

The role of software in Japanese companies increases as automation increases. For example, today roughly 40 percent of the expense of the equipment for automating a factory is software cost. In one Mitsubishi factory where FA facilities are produced, software comprises 70 percent of the total cost of the FA facilities. CIM further increases the relative portion of software cost because of the use of databases and networks. As a result, managing software cost is extremely important with FA and CIM production. This is so true that the focus of advanced cost management is moving from the hardware to the software.

Japan's Software Development Environment

Developing FA or CIM software is a complex process. In addition to determining the needs of the customer, the needs of departments such as manufacturing engineering, product development, manufacturing and marketing must also be unified. Deliveries must be made on time, and quality and service guaranteed. In this sense, the development of FA or CIM software is a joint activity of engineering, manufacturing and marketing.

The Japanese software development environment, in comparison with that in the United States, has the following three notable characteristics:

1. Cooperative Work

U.S. software developers emphasize originality. So, in comparison with Japan, U.S. managers rely more on input by individuals than they do on the contribution of a team. U.S. software development certainly makes maximum use of individual creativity and is widely admired by the Japanese.

Japanese software development is the result of cooperative work of many software engineers. A developer not only gets cooperation from other members of the team, but also obtains the cooperation of others from different departments. Moreover, since it is important for software developers to understand fully the needs and to obtain the cooperation of customers, they frequently cooperate with each other. Japanese software developers analyze requirements and specifications as groups, rather than as individuals. In sum, one of the main characteristics of companies in Japan is that they rely on the creativity of the group rather than on the originality of an individual.

2. Custom Software

Japanese companies prefer custom software developed for a specific purpose rather than general-purpose packaged software from external sources. Whereas in the United States packaged software comprises 50 to 60 percent of all sales, the percentage of packaged software in Japan is very small. In 1991, custom software and system integration accounted for 78 percent of the Japanese software market, compared to 39 percent in the United States.

Japan has little international market presence in the software field. Industry analysts remain divided over where Japanese firms currently stand in the software field (Cusumano, 1991). On one hand, some reports continue to claim the Japanese are years behind the United States. On the other hand, there are increasing reports of high productivity and quality in Japanese software. Japanese firms display enormous creativity in other areas of engineering and possess many abilities that should be of benefit in computer programming.

Both views are partly true. Japanese companies are strong in the *process* of FA applications software such as the steel industry, numerical control machine tools and industrial robots. This is in contrast to the United States, which is very strong in the *product* of packaged software as well as basic system software (for example, Microsoft, Oracle, Novell, Computer Associates, etc.).

The key to FA is software. Logically, therefore, the Japanese must have the expertise to produce the FA software.

3. Software Houses

In Japan, much of the FA and CIM software is developed by software houses. These software houses are typically subsidiaries either of the computer mainframe manufacturers or the companies that use the software, or they are independent subcontractors. This use of outside software developers would be very expensive in the United States, but in Japan it is just the opposite. In strong contrast to their U.S. counterparts, Japanese employees do not like specializing—in anything—because it hinders chances for promotion. Even in management ranks the cross-trained or multifunction (*tanoukou*) worker is the ideal. Those employees who do specialize migrate to specialist firms and accept lower pay. Thus, it is possible to use outside consultants at lower expense than internal employees. This way of getting the services also solves the difficult personnel problems that would come from permanently assigning employees to specialist operations such as computers, which would effectively end their career.

Because of these three special characteristics of Japanese software development, cost management for software in Japan in focused on managing each software order as a whole, and these orders are often entrusted to external personnel who have a detailed reporting obligation.

The Characteristics of
Cost Accounting for Software

Is cost accounting necessary for software and, if so, what kinds of cost accounting systems are used? How many companies use cost accounting systems?

The Software Industry Is a Manufacturing *Industry*

Many experts who develop software in Japan consider the information services industry to be a manufacturing industry. This is the major reason why the Japanese adopted the word "factory" for the place software is developed. Thus it is only natural that more than two-thirds of Japanese software houses use cost accounting for software. Japanese companies have also adopted the factory *approach* to software management. So, it is only natural that most software developers believe that a cost accounting system for software is essentially the same as that for industrial products—even though there are several technical and conceptual differences.

Characteristics of Software Costs

Software costs have some unique characteristics. One is that work in process has no physical substance. As a result, managing software costs is more difficult than managing hardware costs. In addition, for cost management it has become very important to measure properly the number of labor hours spent in developing software.

The second characteristic of software costs is that the cost structure for software is very different from that of hardware. Labor cost is very high, much as it was for manufacturing before automation.

One of the driving forces behind the cost accounting systems is that many software developers need to provide full cost information for reimbursement under the common cost-plus contracts. Only 18 percent of developers use direct costing (variable costing), and the remaining 82 percent of the software houses use absorption costing. The form of absorption costing is more extreme than would be seen in the U.S. manufacturing systems. Their methods calculate the full absorption cost by adding even sales and general administrative expenses to manufacturing costs either regularly (51 percent) or when necessary under production contracts (31 percent). This practice differs markedly from manufacturing companies, which do not continually calculate full absorption costs. However, it is similar to the methods used by defense suppliers.

Cost Management Tools for Software

The major tools for cost management in software development include standard costing, budgeting, target costing and TQC.

Standard Costing

Software development is labor intensive work. This suggests that standard costing can be an effective tool for controlling development cost. In fact, many Japanese mainframe manufacturers use standard costing for controlling system software costs.

Time and motion studies, which are effective in industrial production, cannot be applied to software development because developing software is an intellectual operation that changes from project to project. Thus, Japan's mainframe manufacturers often use cost models to set standards instead of attempting to use work measurement methods. For example, the following standard is set for direct labor costs, input costs and machine costs for a typical software developer.

Standard direct labor costs   = The standard wage rate × the standard labor hours

Standard direct input costs   = The standard entry unit cost × the standard entry hours

Standard direct machine costs = Standard CPU rate × the standard machine hours

However, some factors hinder the adoption of standard costing. First, software is not a mass-produced product. It is produced individually. Thus setting a standard cost for each program takes time and is very difficult. Second, standardization is difficult because the skills of systems engineers vary widely across individuals. Third, software engineering techniques are improving rapidly. In addition, once a standard is set, it becomes behaviorally fixed and work group flexibility is likely to be lost. This could threaten the future development of software technology, and would certainly slow it down in many companies. Standard costing is thus a two-edged sword, which must be considered carefully before implementation.

Budgeting and Progress Management

The core of the manager's control of software development is self-regulated management with profit goals and cost targets. In other words, management sets the overall profitability targets, but leaves the details to the lower-level managers and employees. It relies on the quality and training of the employees to innovate their way to good performance. Software developers must use profit planning and budgeting for this purpose. A profit plan should be prepared first, cost targets set next, then software developed efficiently to achieve the profit goal and cost targets. Performance should be compared between the results that could be obtained and the goal and targets.

It is necessary to check development progress against the schedule by using a budgetary control trend chart. The comparison between the budget and actual results should be conducted at the overall project level, the intermediate levels, and for sub-sub-systems. Figure 18, a cost item control table, is an example of a trend chart.

Cost management linked with progress management of software development work is a part of budgetary control for software development. Budgeting plays an important role in effective project management for most developers. However, progress management with the budget system is not as easy as it might seem.

When product development is behind schedule, even in only one module, the entire operation will probably be delayed. This adds costs. In addition, changes in the external environment (mainly in the marketing, such as changed lead time, features or operational requirements, etc.) and changes in internal environment (mainly man-

Cost	April 199x to March 199x		
	April 199x	Cumulative Total	Forecast
Labor Cost			
Purchase Cost of SW			
Contract Costs			
Computer Costs			
Supplies			
Travel Expenses			
etc.			

Figure 18.   Control chart cost elements
Adapted from: Sakurai, Michiharu, and Paul Scarbrough, Integrated Cost Management, *Productivity Press 1995. Used with permission.*

agement conditions such as transfers of personnel, a new project, delay in operations, lack of appropriate experience by software engineers, etc.) will necessitate changes in planned costs. In this situation it is important to compare actual with planned figures to determine what the effect on profits will be. It is no exaggeration to say that progress management for each operation is the heart of cost management for software.

It is sometimes difficult to estimate revenues and costs when working on a sub-task such as system design, detail design, or testing. In such case, one must always proceed from the premise that the estimated costs may change due to changes in design and operating requirements. Normally, software developers have hundreds of orders and for most projects personnel will be reassigned regularly due to changes in shipping dates desired by customers, delays in the development of hardware, delays in internal company operations, etc. Consequently, planned costs may change. Thus, it is necessary periodically (usually every three months) to compare actual costs with the budget and to modify and revise the budget. It is also essential to trace the variations in costs in the budget systematically from the time of estimation to the time of actual shipping and to identify the cause of the variations. Typical reasons for increases in costs include mistaken estimates and failures in operations due to lack of personnel expertise.

Target Costing for Computer Software

One promising tool in cost management for software is target costing. When a software contract is discussed with a customer, the developer forecasts the sales price. Target profit can be computed from the forecast sales price. Japanese software development houses typically use ROS goals for backing into the target profit. Allowable cost can be computed by subtracting the target profit from the forecast sales price.

While calculating the estimated cost for each feature and process, cost reduction is always the goal. After cost-reduction activities have been tried, the drifting cost is calculated and compared with the allowable, or target cost. When the drifting cost is larger than the allowable cost, it is once again subjected to cost-reduction efforts. If the drifting cost cannot be lowered to the target, then negotiations to raise the price may be necessary. In calculating the drifting cost, modules of code that can be converted or made into general-purpose modules will be taken into account. The ability to convert or reuse parts of an existing program is a major point where cost management for software and hardware differ.

TQC

Since software is developed through the teamwork of many different people, total quality control (TQC) is one of the most effective means of managing it. TQC was introduced to Japanese manufacturing companies at the beginning of the 1970s but its use in software development came much later, in the early 1980s. TQC for software began around 1980 in Japanese mainframe manufacturers. From about this time both NEC and Toshiba aggressively began to develop unique types of TQC. In NEC it is called software quality control (SWQC).

Conclusion

In this chapter we have compared the characteristics of Japanese and U.S. software development and then overviewed cost accounting for software. The reason for this overview is that in order to manage software costs effectively, it is essential to establish a cost management system.

Standard costing is important to control the costs of software development, and what is most important for Japanese companies is project management with a budget. In developing software, work delays lead to delays in shipping that ultimately raise costs. No management measure now available is superior to budgetary planning and control in identifying rising costs.

The human resource management elements that influence software development are also great. Improving individual abilities with training and teamwork is indispensable in solving the problems of individual differences in ability. TQC, which most effectively promotes self-education and mutual education, is an activity most appropriate for Japanese companies, and absolutely essential in software development.

Our final comment on cost management for software concerns target costing. At present no established implementation doctrine describes target costing for software development. Yet, when one considers the possibilities for management, target costing has the potential to become an indispensable tool for strategic cost management, since it can focus the different abilities and experiences of the workers on the goal of profit planning and overall cost reduction—a goal subtly but critically different from that provided by traditional tools.

VII.

ROI vs. ROS:
PERFORMANCE EVALUATION
FOR HIGH-TECHNOLOGY
COMPANIES

J APANESE AND U.S. COMPANIES evaluate performance differently. U.S. company management places great emphasis on return on investment (ROI). ROI is particularly important information for investors in deciding on investments. In contrast, Japanese management generally place greatest emphasis on periodic income. Before the oil crisis of 1973, that tendency was particularly striking. In addition to weak stockholder's strength, companies enjoyed large capital gains in this high-economic growth period by actively investing capital, even if the ROI was low.

Recently, however, high-technology companies have shifted to using the return on sales (ROS) method. This change appears closely related to the slow economic growth and keen competition among companies since 1973. The movement to ROS has been hastened by the five Japanese business innovations, in particular, the job rotation practice that aids the process.

Many U.S. companies, in particular, divisionalized companies, have used ROI since Dupont originated the technique in the 1920s. Three reasons predominate for using ROI: first, most people can understand ROI easily. Second, it combines three critical performance measure variables—sales, earnings and investment. Third, it is popular with financial analysts, investors, creditors and other external information users. Its main flaw is that division managers are apt to reduce investment on R&D and equipment because the investment comes several periods before the return. Also, the size of the investment becomes less and less measurable the more it is divided up among departments, or products.

In contrast, Japanese managers normally evaluate divisional performance in ways beyond measures of profits. They do this because they place great importance on employees and banks, as well as on investors. Relatively few companies have a divisional form of organization, unlike what we see in the United States. Instead, large companies have many subcontractors and other affiliated companies. Consequently, when comparing performance measurement systems, the Japanese need to examine not only divisions but also affiliated companies. The most prevalent form of measuring profit has been periodic income.

There are three main reasons Japanese managers use periodic income to evaluate divisions and affiliated companies:

1. The tendency of ROI to slow down the motivation to invest:

Return on investment = Return on Sales × Turnover, or

$$\frac{\text{Income}}{\text{Investment}} = \frac{\text{Income}}{\text{Sales}} \times \frac{\text{Sales}}{\text{Investment}}$$

2. *Institutional differences:* In the United States, because the stockholders hold great power, earnings per share and ROI dominate. In Japan, on the other hand, proportionately little equity capital exists and therefore the stockholders have little power and short-term goals do not get emphasized. Furthermore, the Japanese tend to take a long-term view of manager performance. This tendency has roots in the lifetime employment tradition as well as the job rotation practice.

   In the United States, ROI finds greater use for performance evaluation than for setting a company's goals. Japanese managers, on the other hand, place greater emphasis on ROI when setting long-range goals than when evaluating performance. Typical Japanese managers find ROI important in formulating long- or middle-range business plans, though they make little use of ROI for short-run business operations.

3. *Rapid economic growth:* In high-growth economic conditions, it is natural to invest aggressively in order to increase sales volume, even with new investments that may exert an adverse effect on

short-term profitability or ROI. During rapid economic expansion, those companies that grew slowly even with high ROI eventually disappeared. Furthermore, there was little or no pressure from stockholders. Thus, for many Japanese companies the best corporate goal was to expand sales volume, market share and income. As for profits, most companies aimed to increase ordinary income—the amount of profits after deducting interest.

ROI vs. ROS

Problems with ROI

In the 1980s economic growth slowed dramatically. The structure of manufacturing continues to evolve rapidly from large scale heavy industry to lighter, smaller scale manufacturing, employing the highest and most advanced technology. The life cycle of consumer products has been radically shortened, as has the life cycle of manufacturing equipment. Although the use of periodic income may have been appropriate for measuring the performance of large-scale heavy industry, it may not be an appropriate measure for evaluating the performance of advanced industry where technology continuously improves.

Problems with ROS

The case against ROS is clear. As we see in the formula on page 83, the turnover or the efficiency of capital is not included in the ROS formula, so that ROS is an incomplete measure of performance for overall evaluation.

Reasons for Using ROS

Most Japanese companies that have proceeded with automation place primary emphasis on ROS for strategic cost management. Are the companies that stress ROS being managed without concern for the efficiency of capital? While the companies that use ROS do so for different reasons, the following are common reasons:

1. Using ROS when a variety of products are produced makes the profitability of each product clear.

2. When a company is using target costing it is easier to set target costs and prices for a variety of products. For example, if a four million yen automobile is ordered and the target profit is 20 percent, then the target profit will be calculated as 800,000 yen (4,000,000 × 0.2).

3. It is nearly impossible to justify the cost of attempting to compute the ROI on each product when producing a small volume of a variety of products.

4. The life cycle of equipment is very short in high-technology industries, so the amount of capital is likely to vary from period to period in these industries. As a result, ROI cannot be reasonably calculated.

5. Large investments of capital are generally needed in order to produce profitable products in high-technology industries. When one relies on ROI, however, desirable investments undertaken for the future are likely to be shown as unprofitable right now.

6. If demand is stable and there is no apprehension about declines in sales, ROI may be effectively employed. However, these conditions do not exist for high-technology products.

7. If there is either hardly any, or absolutely no, pressure from stockholders, then there is little need for ROI.

Hitachi has long considered ROI an important goal. But in 1979 it began evaluating performance according to ROS, with the Dupont performance evaluation index:

$$T(ROI) = U(ROS) \times K(turnover)$$

By evaluating divisions or subsidiaries with the U rank (ROS), Hitachi could easily measure the profitability and competitiveness of each factory against the others. In the corporate headquarters, on the other hand, "T" (ROI), which depends on the overall index is emphasized.

Although we speak of companies making ROS the target, that does not mean that they are managing their companies ignoring the efficiency of capital. For example, such companies as Toyota and Matsushita try to increase their efficiency of capital in a format separate from ROS.

We should remember that JIT is an effective tool for reducing inventory, the most important asset to be managed. Crucial to the asset-management activity is the job-rotation practice, which creates a cadre of extremely knowledgeable midlevel managers capable of making asset turnover increase.

Strategic Use of ROS

In the debit side of the balance sheet the assets are classified roughly as, (1) cash and accounts receivable, (2) inventories, and (3) plant and equipment. Japanese companies cannot expedite the recovery of accounts receivable without the risk of losing sales because terms of payment are customarily determined and exceedingly difficult to change. Reducing investment in fixed assets in order to pay high current dividends may appear advantageous to stockholders, but robs the company of its future. Thus, the critical asset among the three to reduce is inventories.

Why did Toyota originate the JIT system? Both the JIT and target costing are intimately related to using ROS to set target profit. Since the only assets suitable for reduction in the Japanese situation are inventories, it becomes indispensable that inventories be reduced when using ROS. Thus, we see that Toyota's JIT is a policy designed to increase the efficiency of capital through reducing inventories, a specific form of assets. Similarly, Matsushita's internal capital/internal interest system and standard balance sheet is also a means for increasing the efficiency of capital use that is similar to residual income (RI). The ability to increase efficiency of asset use depends on the network of business practices which deliver able, focused, and effective managers to the front line.

In this way the defects of ROI can be reduced by separating it into ROS and asset turnover. When thinking in this fashion, ROS becomes an effective means of management in the age of CIM.

Conclusion

Needless to say, although companies need high ROI in the long run, many companies managed by ROI have lost market share. The defects in ROI are not in the construction of the metric, but in its use by managers. As has often been pointed out, using ROI has also retarded investment in R&D. If Japan had not invested in new markets, expanded its facilities or renewed its equipment because of the substantial costs, and hence a lowering of ROI, it would not be as successful today.

We do not mean to argue that Japanese management has been absolutely correct up to this point. The Japanese tendency to ignore ROI may have artificially intensified domestic and international competition among companies. In addition, as economic growth in Japan slows and inflation dies down, the attitude of managers with respect to capital investment becomes conservative. Also, methods of obtaining capital have expanded to include numerous sources of funds, mainly equity capital. We predict that Japanese managers will become more conscious of ROI than in the past.

However, in high-technology companies, since the oil crisis, ROS rather than ROI has been increasingly used to set target profit. More and more, leading Japanese companies do not use ROI, and thus avoid its underlying faults.

Having considered the above, we argue that *the strategic use* of ROS originated by Toyota should be considered a management innovation along with the well-known ROI of Dupont, and the residual income (RI) of General Electric.

The crucial thing to remember is that the Japanese business environment enabled ROS to function by having such an intense *operating* focus on asset management that they could reduce the *financial* focus on the asset base. The Japanese pay even more attention to the size of the investment and its effectiveness than typical Western firms, and they do it in a different way.

FURTHER READING

Band, Robert E., & James A. Hendricks, "Justifying the Acquisition of Automated Equipment," *Management Accounting,* July 1987, p. 45. [195]

Cusumano, Michael, *Japan's Software Factories: A Challenge to U.S. Management,* Oxford University Press, 1991, pp. 6–7, 47, 51.

FA Report, *Magazine for FA & CIM,* October 1992, pp. 22–25. FA Report, Analysis of Mail Survey on CIM, Magazine for FA & CIM, February 1994, p. 10.

Howell, Robert A., and Stephen R. Soucy, "Capital Investment in the New Manufacturing Environment," *Management Accounting,* Joint Study by NAA & CAM-I, NAA, 1987, pp. 22, 36, 145.

Howell, Robert A., James D. Brown, Stephen R. Soucy and Allen H. Seed III, Management Accounting in the New Manufacturing Environment, A Joint Study by NAA and CAM-I, 1987, pp. 41 and 45.

Japan Industrial Robot Manufacturers Association, *The Present State of and Outlook for Industrial Robots,* October 1992, p. 16.

Kagono, T. I., Nonaka K. Sakakibara and A. Okumura, *Strategic vs. Evolutionary Management, A U.S.-Japan Comparison of Strategy and Organization,* North-Holland, 1985, pp. 37 and 153.

Koenig, Daniel T., *Computer Integrated Manufacturing, Theory and Practice,* Hemisphere Publishing Corporation, 1990, p. 187.

Polakoff, Joel C., "Computer Integrated Manufacturing: A New Look at Cost Justifications," *Journal of Accountancy,* Vol. 169, March 1990, p. 28.

Sakurai, Michiharu, Japan Accounting Association Special Committee, "How Cost Management System Should be Constructed in the New Business Environment," *Integrated Cost Management,* Proceedings of 1993 Japan Accounting Association, September 1993, pp. 1–91. Committee members are the following: Sakurai, Michiharu, chairman (Senshu University), Asada Takayuki (Tsukuba University), Itoh, Yoshihiko (Seikei University), Ogura, Noboru (Tohoku University), Kobayshi, Noritake (Keio University), Satoh, Yasuo (Housei University), Tsuji, Masao (Waseda University), Hiromoto, Toshiro (Hitotsubashi University), Matsuda, Shuichi (Yokohama National University), Monden, Yasuhiro (Tsukuba University), Itoh, Kazunori (Tamagawa Gakuen University).

Sakurai, Michiharu, and Paul Scarbrough, *Integrated Cost Management,* Portland, Oregon: Productivity Press, 1995.

ABOUT THE AUTHORS

Michiharu Sakurai is professor of accounting in the School of Business Administration at Senshu University, Tokyo. He has published many books in Japanese and many articles in Japanese as well as English. Professor Sakurai is one of the most prominent Japanese accounting academics. In 1993 he was voted the most creative and active accounting professor in Japan. He has received many academic awards and serves on many government and industrial committees.

Paul Scarbrough is associate professor of accounting and finance at Brock University in St. Catharines, Ontario, Canada. Professor Scarbrough has worked on Japanese cost management issues for many years and has published articles and a book on this subject.

Dr. Paul Scarbrough, Department of Accounting and Finance, Brock University, St. Catharines, Ontario L2S 3A1 CANADA